THE WEIGHT OF IT ALL

THE WEIGHT OF IT ALL

POETRY BY
MARYAM RIZVI

The Weight of It All
© 2025 Maryam Rizvi
ISBN: 979-8-9987811-8-6

Published by Youth Writer's Press
Colton, California
youthwriterspress.com

First Edition, 2025

To request permissions, you may contact the Publisher at
info@youthwriterscamp.com

Printed in the United States of America.

Cover design by Maryam Rizvi & Emily Anne Evans
Layout design by Emily Anne Evans / Photon Moment LLC

For those who feel alone
In a world full of lonely fighters.

Contents

Foreword

I am honored and ecstatic to be writing this foreword for my daughter. Years ago, when Maryam was in first grade, she finished writing her first poem in the car. I was delighted and overjoyed when I read it. As time goes by, her love for expressing her thoughts through poetry grows and evolves, and her writing becomes ever more meaningful.

Words cannot describe how proud I am of Maryam for sharing her thoughts to the world in *The Weight of It All.* I am ever so eager to watch my daughter grow as a poetess and an incredible human being. It is a great deal to have the courage to share one's thoughts and creativity with others. I hope that Maryam's dear readers will no longer feel alone and lost in their pain after experiencing her poetry.

—Mom

THE WEIGHT
OF IT ALL

Monster

It's hard not to love that which detaches me
From reality,
Like your ability
To create wondrous worlds that spark serenity.

Your brain rests on a pedestal,
For the world to stand in line
To see your musical.
Men lose their pride
When they witness your work's shrine.

They came and went,
But I stayed in the theater,
Unable to measure my heart's meter,
As I watched your musical cease
And heard your diabolical plea:

To remain in your life,
To vow as a wife;
But I can't run to your arms,
I can't be entranced by your charms,

When I've seen past your musical's veneer,
When I've seen past your facade.
Seeing your sinful eyes leer,
Proof from these marks not given by God.

And yet, I cannot leave.
As you walk up to my seat,
I grieve
For what could've been, for feeling defeat.

The art remains in Heaven,
But the artist goes elsewhere.
Yet your existence is a beautiful nightmare.

The brain is separate from the beholder;
My voice is never seen by the critic's eye.
I hurt as your hand wipes my tears —
A silent cry.

Is it so wrong to love a monster?
I crave the need to not even ponder.

Tabula Rasa

Those in charge
Want a world
Where we are all *favorably* unique.

Because the identity belonging to me is,
Respectfully,
Loud and foreign.

So I am stripped of my ancestry and DNA,
Melanin and all,
My being and remaining years
Now a blank slate
To be painted;
My mind,
Having to relearn what is deemed right
By looking at those around me;
Yet they are now the same as I,
Alive souls void of life.

And when I'm cracked and aged,
I'll step out of my house —
One out of many in the world —
Residing on the fine line
Between life and death,
Where we are not quite alive but never dead.
So as I pray on this line,
I wait only for my grays to turn white,
To finally rid me of this absence of a life.

Ana Mendieta

Claimed by neither man nor woman,
But by the earth itself.

The land her abode,
The ocean her unexplored euphoria.

Concealed by the willow of society,
Her identity unknown;
Its roots grasping her tight,
Knowing her voice is larger than life.

Yet her presence is always there,
In every breath we take;
And her message—
Within it,
The blood and agony of the silenced.

Her words and art of the purest intent,
Yet contaminated
By the permanent stain of her misery—
By the loss of her home,
Her life,
Herself.

For amidst the burning skies,
The echoes of her anguish are heard;
Her screams,
To the ignorant and unchanging;
And her tears,
For the sufferers and the unknown.

Heretic

Torrential rains I pray for—
To extinguish the Hell
Igniting beneath my feet.

I long for
A vow of everlasting existence
To be uttered by God,
So any remembrance of me
Isn't carried away by the wind
As my ashes will be.

Heads turn to watch me
As mine tilts towards the Heavens—
Which have seen faces like mine;
With trembling mouths
That have whispered fallacies,
And faltering eyes,
Tears from which only strengthen
The fire of the onlookers—

Who, in a moment's time,
Will experience what they desire;
My sinful existence
Reduced to an event of the past,
Removed from this Earth
And brought down
To the Hellfires.

She, the Ideal

Since birth, they've wanted me to be like her.

They've taught me to be like her.

She who finds life to be the most attractive.

She who doesn't loathe the inevitable.

She who doesn't mourn the temporary.

She who doesn't rely on false contentment.

She who doesn't need validation to be heard.

She who doesn't feel the need to hide.

She who doesn't find comfort in the acts.

She who is eternally confident.

She who isn't suffocated by silence.

She who doesn't exist.

What Have I Given Myself?

What have I given myself
Other than mere subsistence?

Other than countless, elapsing weeks
Of wallowing in regret
And leaning on vain vows
That ignite meaning in the moment
But extinguish the next day?

What have I given myself
Other than an unconscious brain
And pitiful soul
Muddled in coexistence?

Other than anguishing pains
Upon staring at my reflection,
Then emergence into a loveless void?

What have I given myself
Other than the sorrow
Of secluding my being
From those who love me?

Those who reconstruct my shattered body
After I collapse in on myself,
And those who twirl sticks with callused hands
To rekindle the weakening embers of my soul?

Transient

How is it
That I find beauty
In every version of myself
That does not exist,
Yet
I can never find it
In the existing one?

In an age of answers
Plagued by speed,
And in an age of
Delusive joy
Found in the screen,
I spend my time
Observing trends
As they climb and fall,
And lookalike people
With whom I've no relation at all.

And as my brain soaks it all in,
Wasted hours penetrating through,
My eyes are rinsed in blue,
My mind overcome with realization.

The realization
That I am void of all individuality,
That my tendency
To live through others' chosen moments
Will only resort in my fatality.

The realization
That my days are too numbered,
Too precious,
To remain a stranger
To the flesh I was given.

In Vain

The valiant efforts I have made

To amend my disdainful ways

All go to waste when I hear your voice.

You have failed me numerous times

Throughout these years.

I am enamored by your relentless ways

Of giving only pain

To those who love you.

And although I detest you,

I detest myself more

For continuously pining over you

Despite the bleeding of my fresh wounds,

Graciously provided by your protruding sword.

The Inevitable

The sun can only smile ever so often.
Yet when it's dawn, we yearn for our slumber.
And when it's dusk, we mourn the fleeting light.

Many live this way;
They miss what once was
Without ever having loved it in its presence.

Such as she,
Who now fears she won't see the sun's return,
Who spends her last hours begging at Death's feet —
Vowing to live as she was told,
As moral as one can be.

Praying in between her cries of persistence
To continue living,
All Death can do is look down at her in pity,
Watching her pray against what is
The inevitable.

And ask:
Why do your tears fall now
When your skin has long gone thirsted?
When you're about to leave this existence
Which you so deeply loathed?
Why do you now choose to stay
When all you've wanted is an escape
From all that has pained you?
Why does your vision of freedom change now
When all you've wanted is to rid yourself
Of your shackles?

You've long felt confined to your cave.
Your tears have always seemed to fall
When you say my name —
In the past, and in the present.
You've often wished for my arrival,
For me to give you wings,
So you can fly away to the one sunbeam
Shining into your cave.
What a pity
That only now,
You feel freed from your shackles,
That only now,
Your eyes witness the entire sun
Beyond the cave.

Drowning in Life

Drowning in life,
In the tides of my 50's film,
Living in a way that used to feel normal.

Surrendered to the waves long ago,
Nearly swallowed whole,
Nearly forgotten,
Nearly there
To what felt like the inevitable;

Until you fished me out
With your rose-colored glasses,
Behind which were ebullient eyes,
Vessels of vivacity.

And although I desperately strived
To ignore you,
To immobilize you,
To prevent you
From interfering with my fate,
From convincing me of your vain lie,

I could not leave you
Knowing your film was more vivid than mine.
I could not stray you away
Knowing even your facade of a lie was better
Than mine.

And although I never left you,
Although I examined you,
Studied you,
Breathed you,

I could not understand why
Or how
You are the way you are,
You live the way you do.

I felt as if the hours were slipping by,
As if the film was coming to an end,
As if the tides would swallow me whole,
Like that moment all over again.

So I stole your glasses
And peered through them,
Hoping I could escape my fate.

But the tint was no longer.
It had bled
Into your mind and body,
Leaving not a trace.

How miserably I tried
To claw my way inside you,
To find rose-colored blood
And smear it on my face,
Praying it would stain me
Like how the tint had stained you.

But I remained the same,
And so did you.

And now,
As the waves are approaching,
As I am about to be swallowed whole,
As I am about to be forgotten,
As I am nearly there
To what may really be the inevitable,
I pray there will be a rose on the ocean floor —
One of my very own —
To stain me
As yours had stained you.

Stained Hands

Once so tall,
He used to look down at those below
From the summit of pride—
A feat praised
By the vengeful and bloodthirsty.

Now, cowering,
His face a mixture
Of streams of tears
And another's life,
His body faltering and limp,
As if he were trying to die
In place of the soldier he was struggling
To save.

Men, they both were—
Terrified and starved,
Wishing to be introduced
To the inevitable End.

Alike, they both were—
The only difference being the homicidal, Vengeful liars
They had pledged themselves to.

Blood escaping with each struggling gasp,
He failed to impede the flow of love and age
From the man's tense, failing body.

A body turned corpse,
As the faltering gasps ceased—
A look of duality in his now soulless eyes:
One of fear for the fleeting of life
And the other of peaceful acceptance of
The End.

But
Even amidst the once-harrowing explosions
Of gunfire,
The victim's silence was deafening,
And the man couldn't seem
To take his stained hands
Off his corpse.

Blanketed Memories

The sandstorm approaching on the horizon
Will bring an impending, perpetual hush
On the still-ransacked minds
Of these martyred soldiers.

As for myself,
Even God's embrace
Wouldn't extinguish the murderous guilt
Gnawing at my insides
From the countless sins
I have thoughtlessly committed.

Lying next to the rifle
That had fallen from my grasp
As I had lost life in my hand and faltered,
My eyes betray my thoughts —
As if with a soul of their own —
And focus on the bullet wound
Of the man ahead,
An abyssal rupture of crimson
Bleeding anew
On his long-stained uniform.

If only our eyes had met,
For he could have seen
The repenting weight my eyes bore
Before life left him.

An otherworldly whistle
Intensifies as the sands draw nearer,
Like Death is calling out my name.

Mother Nature —
With your charred hands of loss and grief,
Do one final service for these men,
And blanket them
With what is left of your trodden,
All-too-familiar soil;
The same soil we've shed innocent blood on.

The sands blow over the bled-dry carnage —
As if to shield them,
As if to protect them,
To act as a grave.

I pray
That not long after
The pain of our absence subsides,
Joy and laughter
Will suffuse this land,
Like the appearance of the rocket flowers
In Kabul.

Mural of Self

Residing in an eternally-isolated room
With what were once blank canvases,
The walls are now resuscitated with color
As I aimlessly smear paint.

A green and white flag on the ceiling
With an ambitious girl
Straining on its crescent moon,
Tirelessly reaching for a single star.

And below her,
Roaring ocean waves,
Never idle nor calm,
Overwhelming the eye with uninvited change And
emotion.

Illuminating them is the sun,
For whose rays I yearn —
Despite how dim they may be —
When I'm shrouded
In the marine-colored depths.

These unending tides
Crash against overarching mountains and cliffs,
Jagged and weary with years of tear,
But built by effort and resilience,
Emblems of achievement and possibility.

Yet,
Distracting from the colors of truth,
A shadow,
A hole,
Looms over
In the middle of it all.

Innate confusion
And caution
Infused within my brain,
It is difficult to paint
What has not yet become reality.

But,
Alas,
As the years travel by,
As the next star is reached for,
As the waves incessantly crash,
As the sun routinely rises,
And as the mountains are climbed,
This room will remain the same,
And the time will come
To bring light
To the shadow.

Truth

The truth is,

Poets are not poetic.

Life is.

Poets are mindless.

Life is what feeds them.

Relentlessly, it throws

Moments at me

That are

Raw and bare,

And so heavy

That they hurl me into

The ocean of lifeless voids,

Where I drown

And disappear into the nameless depths.

Yet it shows me

That even the slightest essence of beauty

Is extracted from those moments,

That even the depths have an end.

Acknowledgements

First and foremost, I want to thank Brandon Allen for giving me the opportunity to achieve such a high and cherished milestone — one that I have kept in the back of my mind for such a long time. When I began writing poetry at a younger age, I did so purely for the amusement and joy creative writing brought me. Never would I have guessed that I would one day strive to make my work known and seen by those who need it the most, and I am beyond thankful to you for opening the door to making my aspirations a reality.

I am indebted and eternally grateful to my mother and father, who have inspired and motivated me throughout this journey of self-discovery before I was even aware I was on it. I would not have achieved what I have if it were not for your nurturing of my passions and talents, and for the warm comfort you have given me in my own times of self-hatred and pain. I owe much of my joy and confidence to you. Thank you for each and every sacrifice you have made for me, and for the support you have given me — as parents, as mentors, and as friends.

About the Author

Maryam Rizvi's strong passion for poetry began in the first grade, when she discovered she could bring pen to paper to creatively express her thoughts and dreams for the future (which were usually about running away to Paris). Over time, poetry became a refuge for her, a way to cope with daily distresses and to bring comfort in times of grief. Today, she continues writing — for the sake of others in need of solace, and to raise awareness for the voiceless.

youthwriterspress.com

A program of Youth Writer's Camp, Inc., Youth Writer's Press exists to create a safe space where young voices are heard, valued, and amplified. We are dedicated to producing and publishing work that allows youth to share their truths with the world. Our mission is to equip the next generation of writers with the resources, confidence, and platform to turn their stories into lasting works that resound far beyond the page.

youthwriterscamp.com

This book was created as part of Youth Writer's Camp, Inc., a nonprofit organization whose mission is to motivate communities to redefine hope for young people through mentoring, enrichment, and creativity.

In our workshops and programs, we blend literacy enrichment, social-emotional development, and creative entrepreneurship — using writing as a tool for healing, growth, and community connection.

Youth Writer's Camp Values:

COURAGE Creating the strength to face challenges with confidence.

RESILIENCE Creating the ability to bounce back and keep moving forward.

EMPATHY Creating connections by truly understanding others' feelings.

AUTHENTICITY Creating a space where you can be your true self without masks.

TRANSPARENCY Creating an atmosphere of openness and honesty, where vulnerability is valued.

ENTERPRISING Creating opportunities through innovation and a dynamic mindset.